doodle studio

illustrated by Amanda Haley

★ American Girl™

Published by Pleasant Company Publications

Questions or comments? Call 1-800-845-0005,
visit our Web site at **americangirl.com**, or write to
American Girl, P.O. Box 620497, Middleton, WI 53562.

Printed and assembled in China.
Components made in China & the U.S.A.

06 07 08 09 10 C&C 15 14 13 12 11

Editorial Development: Trula Magruder, Michelle Watkins

Art Direction: Chris Lorette David, Camela Decaire

Design: Camela Decaire

Production: Kendra Pulvermacher, Mindy Rappe

Illustrations: Amanda Haley

Photography: Jamie Young

Dear Doodler...

Thousands of girls shared their doodles with us.
Here is a collection of our **favorites** for you to draw
and use to **decorate** all sorts of stuff. Follow the fun
step-by-step directions to learn the doodles. Then use
your doodles to **create** scenes in your doodle diary or
to decorate the **supplies** you'll find inside, including
stickers, T-shirt transfers, magnets, and more!

Your friends at American Girl

There's so much you can do . . .

Sticky Stuff

Draw your favorite doodles on blank **stickers.** Share them with pals or stick them on notebooks, lockers, letters—anywhere! Or doodle on blank **magnets** with markers, then cut out with scissors. Decorate the fridge, your locker, or a metal frame.

T-shirt Transfers

Use permanent markers to create mini doodles on **iron-on transfer paper,** then follow manufacturer's instructions closely.

♡ Ask a parent to help you iron the doodle onto the T-shirt right after you've drawn it, while the ink's still a bit damp.

. . .with doodles drawn by you!

Itty Bitty Doodles
Use markers to draw doodles on **shrinky plastic,** then follow manufacturer's directions. Try using a hole punch to make a hole in the top center of the plastic before baking. When it's cool, string the mini doodle on a jewelry chain.

Spot Art
Save your spot in a book with a doodled **bookmark.** Get fancy and add a **tassel.** Give one as a gift with a favorite book.

Art Journal
Practice and preserve your art in your personal **doodle diary.** Save your special doodles on the blank pages, play with new scenes or ideas, or just practice, practice, practice!

Time to clean up...pup!

Draw two 3's

like this.

Add three
arching lines.

Create ears, eyes,

and a nose.

Ready to
walk and roll!!

Start with
a U.

Wrap a line
from one side

to the other.

Make a stubby body,

stubby legs, and
a stubby tail.

This dog is begging
for fun!

Start with a P.

Add this shape.

make two floppy ears

and a muzzley nose.

Puppy love!

Draw a U.

Make five more like this.

Add three circles.

Fur U.

First make a
kidney bean.

Attach a smaller
kidney bean

like this.

Draw a body, a nose,
legs, and a tail.

See Spot?

See Spot's spot?

Draw a doughnut
with a piece missing.

make a half-circle.

Add ears, eyes,

and front legs.

Sit!

Good boy!

Start with an arch.

Attach a sideways arch

and big and small ovals.

Add a squat body,

feet, and a tail.

"I ain't nothin' but a hound dog..."

Start with a clover.

Add a circle and eyes.

Draw a nose and legs.

Ta-da! A doodled poodle.

Make three U's
Side by side.

Connect the U's and
add
three
Circles.

make a wienie body,
legs, and
a tail.

Every dog has its day!

Cover a Y with an
Upside-down U.

Connect the U to
the Y like this.

Draw a head and
two more legs.

Tail that dog!

Draw a fluffy cloud.

Attach five more.

Add fluffy legs and a tail.

Put a head in the clouds!

Draw an upside-down heart.

Add ears, a face, and dots.

Make a body and legs.

Give him some spots.

The end!

Missing Kitty!

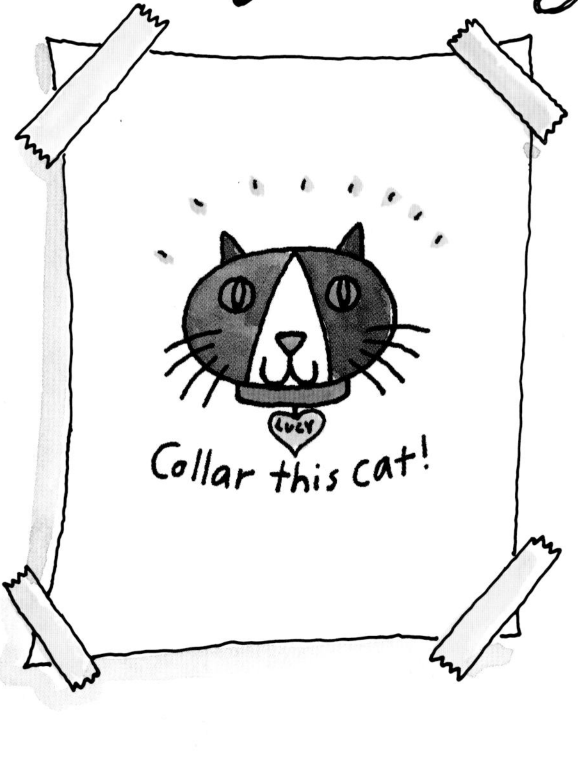

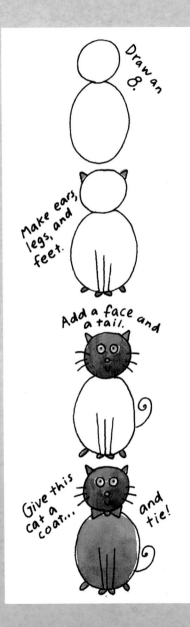

Draw an 8.

Make ears, legs, and feet.

Add a face and a tail.

Give this cat a coat... and tie!

Begin with a C.

Then attach a sideways U.

Make a face, ears, paws, and a curly tail.

"C" the cat wants to play!

Make a
w i d e W.

Attach a half-circle.

Add a face,

legs, and a tail.

Look at that
alley cat!

Draw a kidney bean.

Add a circle and
some small triangles.

Add ears, legs,
and a tail.

Finish with a
purr-fect face!

Draw an a.

Add a circle.

Create ears and some legs.

A real fat cat!

meow!

∧ ∧
Start with two upside-down V's.

Connect the V's and

attach a U.

Draw a body, two paws, and a long tail.

Look what the cat dragged in!

Make an oval.

Rest it on another one.

Add ears, a whiskery face,

legs, and a tail.

Night prowler

Start with an 8.

Add two triangles

and four little circles.

Draw a face, whiskers, and a tail.

Make this kitty pretty.

Doodle Diner

A table for two!

Draw an X.

Add top and bottom lines.

Draw an upside-down U.

Take a crack at a spoon!

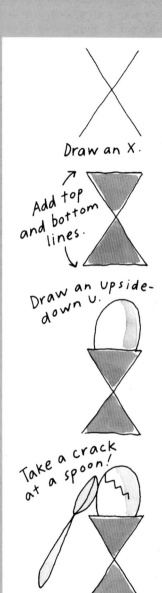

Draw 4 waves close together.

Make a rectangle around each pair.

Put the pair inside an oval.

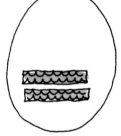

Now you're cookin'!

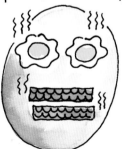

Draw 8 straight lines.

Add lettuce...

...cheese, mayo, or mustard.

A doodle-decker sandwich!

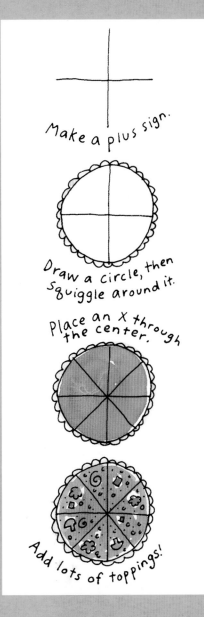

Make a plus sign.

Draw a circle, then squiggle around it.

Place an X through the center.

Add lots of toppings!

Draw a kidney bean.

Make another.

Add lettuce and a plate.

Top with sesame seeds.

Fast food!

Draw a sideways J.

Attach another and create squiggles here.

Add a yummy bun.

This doodle's out to lunch! Soda

Draw 3 itty-bitty B's.

Add a skinny triangle.

Make a piece of pie and a plate like this.

Don't forget the milk!

Draw a smile.

Make shapes like this.

Dribble on chocolate sauce, and plop on a cherry.

Dig in!

Baby Sister

- Picture perfect -

Dream up a moon.

Attach an oval.

Add a face.

Rock-a-bye baby.

Make an 8.

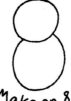

Add a banana shape to each side.

Draw arms, legs, and

a silly face.

Funny bunny!

make an oval.

Add three more.

Draw horns, ears,

and legs.

How now
beanie cow?

Draw 2 X's
in a circle.

Make
a dress.

Create hands
and feet.

Hello, Dolly!

Create a half-circle.

Top with a circle.

Add ears

and a tail.

Let the circus begin!

Start with a b.

Draw this shape.

Make tiny feet, hair,

arms, and hands.

Got the swing of it?

Make an oval.

Attach four more.

And add five more.

Give a dancing bear circus flair.

Draw a d.

Make a four-pointed star like this.

Add hair and clothes to wear.

Reach for a circus treat!

make a clover.

Fill in a circle, ears, and a face.

Add whiskers and a body with legs.

A dandy-lion!

Draw a kidney bean.

Add a head, ears, and a body.

make a hat and hair.

Clown around with a face.

Make a backward C.

Attach an oval.

Draw an eye, an ear,

and legs.

Attach trunks and tails
for an elephant parade.

Start with two
lines running
downhill.

make this shape.

Add a face,

perky ears, and
a broad neck.

Drawing beautiful
hair is the
mane event.

Start with a 4
like this.

Attach an M

with a long tail.

Draw a face and
a mane.

Built 4 speed!

C

First make a C.

Connect the C to a long-tailed M.

Add a face, a mane,

and a horsey neck.

Slip on a bridle,

then giddyap!

Start with a C.

Add ears.

Draw a face and a neck.

Hay, pardner!

Field Trip

Doodle Aquarium →

Draw a sideways
teardrop.

Add some
curls.

Draw a happy
face.

Finish with a
whale of a
tail!

Draw a
B on its
side.

Put a circle
around it.

Add whiskers
and eyes.

Surf's up!

Draw a fish.

Put a circle on top, and add a line here.

Add arms and hair.

Play in the waves!

Draw a star.

Create plants and an ocean floor.

Add a few fish.

Wish upon a Starfish!

Draw a spoon.

Add some lines to make a tail.

Create some fishy fins.

Finish with a face. Bubble up!

Draw a diamond on its side.

Add little circles and a wiggly line.

Design an ocean floor.

Finish with a face. Careful! Don't get stung!

Draw a
lightning bolt.

Add a dot.

Create a body
and scales.

3 3
3 3 3 3 3
3 3 3 3 3

Fish for a
compliment!

3 3 3
3 3 3
3 3 3

"Nice doodle!"

Draw a sideways
heart.

Add a circle and
a small heart.

make an eye, fins,
and scales.

Fat and happy!

friendly Faces

Draw a simple curlicue...

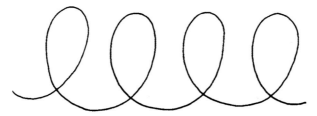

...that turns into a girly-cue!

Draw 2 spoons.

Scribble some hair.

↑
Add a line here.

Here's looking at you, kid!

Draw an upside-down U.

Make a line and a half-circle.

Add hair and a face.

Tie on a bright bandanna, pardner!

× ×
× ×
× ×
× ×
× ×
× ×
× ×

Draw 2
Columns of X's.

Make a U
Shape.

Add bangs and ends.

Finish with a
freckled face.

Draw an e.

Make a line.

Add some hair.

Finish with a face
and freckles, too!

Start with a
Kidney bean.

Draw some hair.

Add a line
here ↓

↖and here.

An American girl
in Paris!

Draw an upside-
down smile.

Add a
U.

Scribble some
hair.

A loud band!

Draw an e.

Scribble in here.

Complete the circle.

Add pigtails and pretty bows.

Doodle a face and dimples, too!

Start with an e.

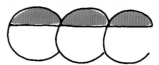

Make 2 more.

Add caps and faces.

Draw hair.

Now that's teamwork!

Start with a circle.

Add a triangle.

Draw a shape like this. ↙

This tiger's a pussycat!

Draw a sideways 8.

Add stumpy legs.

Create a tail and a big ear.

Finish with a shower!

Make a fat L with an open end.

Attach four W's to the bottom.

Draw this head.

Spot a giraffe at the zoo!

Start with a big heart.

Draw a circle inside.

Create a body and a long swishy tail.

meow!

Finish with a face, some ears, and let out a roar!

Start with a
Kidney bean.

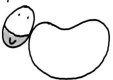

Add a sweet face.

Give her legs to
stand on

and ears to hear.

This zebra's earned
her stripes!

Make a big circle
and a small one!

Connect them.

Add hair, a beak,

and bird feet.

'A' tall tail!'

Draw an upside-down raindrop.

Attach an oval.

Add wings, tail feathers,

and bird feet.

Add eyes, then wet your whistle!

Make a squiggle.

Add a curvy line here.

Attach an oval.

Finish the face and you're over the hump!

Hit the beach!

Start with a spoon.

Add a sun hat and braids.

Give her a bathing suit and a smiling face.

Finish with arms, legs, and a sand castle, too!

Draw a circle

Now make it "bounce!"

Draw a 4.

Happy sailing!

American Girl

S

Start with an S.

Attach this shape. ←

Add a face, a body, a wing, and feet.

Give this pelican a perch.

Draw an M and an N.

Aloha!

Spin a spiral...

...for fun in the sun!

Secret Garden

How does your
garden grow?

Draw two U's.

Add two zigzag tops.

Make two curvy lines.

Best buds!

Begin with a B.

Attach a backward B.

Make a small head with antennae.

You've passed with flying colors!

Draw 3 bows.

Cross each bow with another bow.

Place dots in the middle.

To make bows grow, add stems and leaves.

Draw a heart.

Add another.

Make a body, a head, and antennae, too!

Get carried away with pretty patterns!

Begin with a B

like this.

Attach a half-circle
at the bottom.

Draw ears, a
face, legs, and
a tail.

Add bouncing
baby bunnies!

Draw a U.

Insert a V.

Add a stalk
and leaves.

Autumn harvest.

Start with a circle.

Add lines across it.

Make bee-dy eyes and tiny antennae.

A bee can't buzz without wings.

Draw a heart on its side.

Add a center line and a half-circle.

Make a head, legs, and antennae, too.

Add a smile and spots.
Now fly away home!

Start with a U turned like this.

Add an oval and a tail.

Draw four little legs and a smiling face.

This doodle's a winner!

Start with an oval.

Add a C and five tiny triangles.

Draw four feet and one long tail.

Purrr!

Snuggle up!

Draw four fingers.

Dot each finger.

Add a middle line, four ears,

and two noses.

Bunny buddies!

Draw an oval...

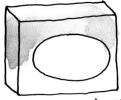

...put it in a box.

Add a little yellow,

and call her Goldilocks!

Draw an upside-down mitten.

Add another thumb.

make a face.

Dress up Dottie for the holidays!

Draw a lightning bolt.

Make a body.

Add eyes, legs, and a tail.

Finish with scary teeth.

grrrr!

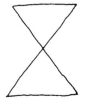

Draw a bow on
its side.

make a tiny face
and whiskers.

Add ears, feet,
and a tail.

Every mouse needs
a house!

Start with a
sideways 8.

Add a
loop →
and two
straight lines.

Wrap legs
around the lines.

Pond picnic!

Down on the Farm

Cock-a-DooDLE-doo!

N N
Draw 2 N's ↑
like this.

Connect the N's here,
↗ W W
and add these lines.

Create a body
with a tail
and face.

Udderly
Sweet!

Draw a cloud.

Make a small
cloud at one end.

Add 4 more puffs
at the bottom.

Wool you be mine?

Start with a heart.

Add bird feet.

Fill in the feathers.

Gobble up this doodle!

Draw two E's

on their sides.

Add these lines.

Attach a head

and a tail.

Here's looking at moo!

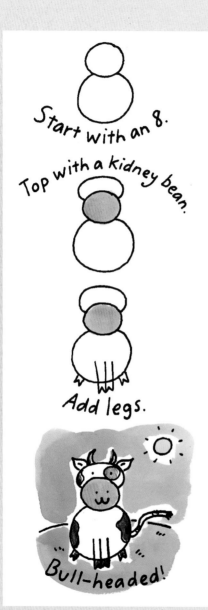

Start with an 8.

Top with a kidney bean.

Add legs.

Bull-headed!

Draw a C and a backward C.

Make zigzags.

Add a head, a body, and a leg.

Happy "bird"-day!

Make an open-ended, fat 6.

Add a V beak, big circle eyes,

and bird legs.

Give this emu something to chew!

Make an h.

Add five ovals.

Draw a face, ears, a mane, and a tail!

Happy trails to you!

Heavenly Doodles

Overlap four big hearts.

Add a halo, a head, hands, and feet. Isn't this angel really sweet?

Make a keyhole.

Put an oval above it.

Add wings and arms.

Voice of an angel!!

Draw 2 mittens.

Make a tube shape like this.

Add a head, arms, and legs.

Your guardian angel.

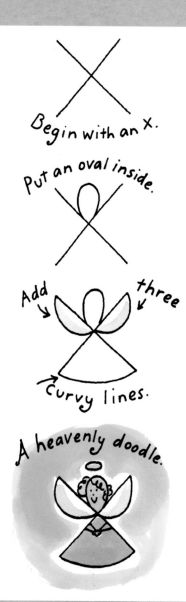

Begin with an X.

Put an oval inside.

Add three Curvy lines.

A heavenly doodle.

Start with an A.

Add a curvy line and a straight one.

Make a head, arms, and a heavenly dress.

"A" guardian angel to watch over U!

The Water's Edge

Queen of the Hop!

9   9
9
Start with 9's.

Add arches and lines.

Draw faces

and feet.

Water babies.

Float a circle
on the page.

Connect an oval
to the circle.

Draw ears,

a whiskery face,
and stumpy feet.

You "otter" add
a tail and a lazy river.

make an S.

Draw a squiggly line over it.

make a big wing,

tail feathers, and feet.

Time to dry. Give a shake to the sky!

Join two cursive L's...

...to a curvy line...

...then make more L's...

...that swirl into a Swan.

make an 8.

Draw a circle in the bottom.

Add a face, legs, and a tail.

Swell shell!

Draw a 4.

make legs with little bird feet.

Create a body and some feathers.

Add a neck and a head, and think pink!

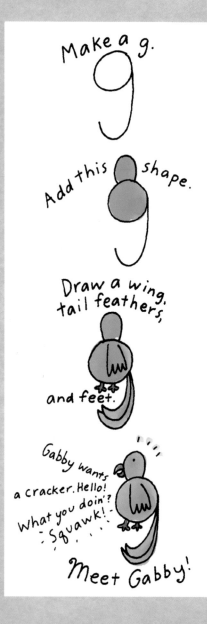

Make a g.

Add this shape.

Draw a wing, tail feathers, and feet.

Gabby wants a cracker. Hello! What you doin'? Squawk!

Meet Gabby!

First make a 2.

Add a circle with a pointed end.

Draw wings.

Lovebirds!

Sweet Dreams

Good night, moon.

Draw two j's.

j   j

Attach them like this.

Add a wave.

Time for bed!

Make a star.

Fatten one side.

Put it on a pole.

Wish upon a star!

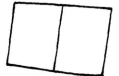

Draw two rectangles.

make a center spiral.

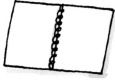

Add a pencil and a light.

Jot in your journal!

Draw a slanted raindrop.

Add a circle and a curvy line.

make a big body.

A favorite friend.

Start with a plus sign.

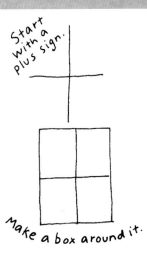

Make a box around it.

Draw curtains with a squiggle here

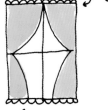

and here.

Finish with stars

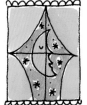

and the light of the silvery moon.

Draw a sideways B.

Add a head, ears, and a face.

Create a feathered body and feet.

'Night, owl!

Draw 2 clovers.

Add legs and pants.

Make ears and whiskers.

Finish with faces. Hop to it!

Draw a bow that slants like this.

Attach a big U to the bottom.

Create hair, a face, and snazzy PJ's.

Choose a perfect pillow pal. Nighty night!